D0794628

DISCARD

THE LOUISIANA PURCHASE THROUGH THE EYES OF THOMAS JEFFERSON

by Anita Yasuda

Content Consultant
John B. Boles, PhD
Professor of History
Rice University

Core Library

An Imprint of Abdo Publishing
abdopublishing.com

abdopublishing.com

Published by Abdo Publishing, a division of ABDO, PO Box 398166, Minneapolis, Minnesota 55439. Copyright © 2016 by Abdo Consulting Group, Inc. International copyrights reserved in all countries. No part of this book may be reproduced in any form without written permission from the publisher. Core Library™ is a trademark and logo of Abdo Publishing.

Printed in the United States of America, North Mankato, Minnesota
082015
012016

THIS BOOK CONTAINS
RECYCLED MATERIALS

Cover Photo: iStockphoto
Interior Photos: iStockphoto, 1, 14; Picture History/Newscom, 4; Aleksandar Nakic/iStockphoto, 6, 45; Album/Oronoz/Newscom, 8; North Wind Picture Archives, 10, 34; US Navy Naval History and Heritage Command, 17; Bettmann/Corbis, 18, 26, 37; Linda Steward/iStockphoto, 22; Everett Historical/Shutterstock Images, 24; Constantino Brumidi, 28; Popperfoto/Getty Images, 32

Editor: Jon Westmark
Series Designer: Laura Polzin

Library of Congress Control Number: 2015945405

Cataloging-in-Publication Data
Yasuda, Anita.
 The Louisiana Purchase through the eyes of Thomas Jefferson / Anita Yasuda.
   p. cm. -- (Presidential perspectives)
 ISBN 978-1-68078-032-1 (lib. bdg.)
 Includes bibliographical references and index.
 1. Louisiana Purchase--Juvenile literature. 2. Jefferson, Thomas, 1743-1826--Juvenile literature.
 3. Presidents--United States--Juvenile literature. 4. United States--Territorial expansion.   I. Title.
 973.4--dc23
                                                                    2015945405

CONTENTS

CHAPTER ONE

THOMAS JEFFERSON'S VISION

Thomas Jefferson had a bold dream for the United States. On March 4, 1801, he took office as the country's third president. At the age of 57, Jefferson already had a long history as a politician. In his first address in the US Capitol in Washington, DC, Jefferson shared his vision. He spoke of "a nation, spread over a wide and fruitful land, traversing all the seas with the rich productions of their industry."

Jefferson had served as state governor, foreign diplomat, secretary of state, and vice president before becoming president in 1801.

Jefferson believed strongly in the US Constitution. He wanted to follow it closely as president.

To accomplish this, Jefferson envisioned the country growing westward.

Jefferson's goals for the nation touched many of those in attendance. At the end of his speech, applause rang out from the crowd of more than 1,000 people. Some of those who were packed into the Senate chamber were moved to tears.

That morning there had not been a fancy carriage ride to the Capitol. Instead, Jefferson had dressed in a plain suit and walked with a small group of people. He felt that this best represented his beliefs. He was not a royal figure. He was a servant of the US people.

In his speech, Jefferson said the US government would be smaller in the future. He was a Democratic-Republican. This meant he did not want the central government to become too powerful. He supported stronger states' rights. His Federalist opponents held the opposite view. During his speech, Jefferson also said the military would be smaller. But his vision for the United States would not be small. It would be bigger than anyone thought possible.

Dreaming of the West

Jefferson's interest in the West started during his childhood. His father was a surveyor, explorer, and mapmaker. Jefferson loved hearing about famous explorers and Native Americans. The stories stayed with him long after he left his childhood home in Virginia.

As an adult, Jefferson kept learning about the West. He studied maps of North America. He learned it was more than 3,000 miles (4,828 km) across.

The wilderness captured Jefferson's imagination.

Throughout the 1780s and 1790s, Jefferson pushed for the land west of the Mississippi River to be explored. He wrote letters to explorers. In 1793 he raised money for a private expedition across the West. But the trip fell through.

As president, Jefferson felt westward growth was key to the future of the United States. More land would allow more Americans to own farms. Jefferson believed Native Americans in the West would benefit from adopting European ways of life. But the nation was small when he took office in 1801. It was a group of states near the Atlantic Ocean. Many countries held lands around the United States. The area west of the Mississippi belonged to Spain. It was known as Louisiana. France gave Spain this land after the French and Indian War (1754–1763). Britain had defeated the French in the war. Spain also controlled land to the south of the United States. This territory was called East and West Florida. Britain held land to the north.

A Crowded Continent

This map shows how North America was divided before 1800. What does it tell you about the size of the United States in comparison to Spanish and British holdings in North America? How does the map help you understand the importance of Louisiana?

The Secret Agreement

Jefferson had not finished his first month in office before he faced a serious threat to his plan for US growth. On March 29, 1801, Jefferson received news about Louisiana from Rufus King. King was an American diplomat in London, England. He wrote that Spain had secretly traded Louisiana and the Floridas to France in exchange for land in Italy. This was a big problem for Jefferson.

In the early 1800s, Louisiana included the land from the Gulf of Mexico to the Great Lakes. It stretched from east of the Mississippi River to the Rocky Mountains. US farmers in the Ohio River Valley relied on the Mississippi for transportation and trade. The United States had an agreement with Spain called the Treaty of San Lorenzo. It allowed Americans to use the river. Jefferson feared that France might stop US trade from New Orleans by closing the Mississippi. He also thought Spain

PERSPECTIVES
The Spanish Point of View

The Spanish did not want to give up Louisiana. But since the end of the American Revolutionary War (1775–1783), more Americans had traveled west. They farmed and traded on Spanish-held lands. Spain felt that Americans were hostile toward Spanish leadership. Spain could not stop American settlers from coming. But they could control the trade through treaties.

The Treaty of San Lorenzo

Spain held the port of New Orleans. The city was key to accessing the Mississippi River. On October 27, 1795, the United States and Spain signed the Treaty of San Lorenzo. The US envoy to Spain, Thomas Pinckney, arranged the treaty. Under it, Americans could float their goods down the Mississippi to New Orleans. From there the goods would be put on ships to travel to ports along the Atlantic coast. The treaty led to more trade. It encouraged more settlers to move west.

was weaker than France. He believed that one day the United States would peacefully take Spanish lands in North America. Louisiana was a big part of this plan.

Napoléon I was the ruler of France. He had come to power in 1799. Jefferson hoped he had no interest in Louisiana. But Napoléon talked of rebuilding a French empire in the Americas. France had held most of North America before the French and Indian War. Jefferson believed if France regained control of the territory, there would be little hope of the United States expanding west.

One of Jefferson's favorite personal expeditions was to a naturally formed rock bridge in Virginia. He described visiting the site in his journal:

> *The Natural Bridge, the most sublime of Nature's works. . . . is on the ascent of a hill which seems to have been cloven through its length by some great convulsion. The fissure . . . is, by some admeasurements, 270 feet [83 m] deep, by others only 205 [62 m]. It is about 45 feet [14 m] wide at the bottom, and 90 feet [27 m] at the top. . . . Looking down from this height about a minute, gave me a violent headache. If the view from the top be painful and intolerable, that from below is delightful in an equal extreme. It is impossible for the emotions arising from the sublime to be felt beyond what they are here: so beautiful an arch, so elevated, so light, and springing as it were up to heaven, the rapture of the spectator is really indescribable!*
>
> Source: Thomas Jefferson. The Writings of Thomas Jefferson. New York: Modern Library, 1944.

Back it up

Jefferson uses his experience to support a point. Write a paragraph describing what point he is making. Then write down two or three things he uses to make the point.

CHAPTER TWO

THE THREAT IS REAL

Jefferson gathered information about Napoléon's activities from newspapers, travelers, and diplomats. He wrote to friends in Europe. Jefferson needed to know if the deal between Spain and France existed.

In November 1801, Jefferson got his answer. King sent him a copy of the Treaty of San Ildefonso. It confirmed the secret France had tried to keep for

Rufus King informed Jefferson of a secret treaty between France and Spain.

almost two years. Louisiana belonged to France. But France had left the Spanish in control.

Jefferson turned to his friend and secretary of state, James Madison, for advice. Madison was ill and unable to be in Washington. He kept in touch with the president through letters. On May 26, 1801, Jefferson wrote to Madison. Jefferson explained that the treaty was unwise for France and Spain and worrying for the United States.

Madison agreed. The British held land to the north. If France began building settlements in North America, the two

The Treaty of San Ildefonso

On October 1, 1800, Napoléon made a deal with Spain. He promised to give the King of Spain's son-in-law a kingdom in Tuscany, where France held land. In return, Spain agreed to return Louisiana to France. The agreement was kept secret. Napoléon worried that if the treaty were announced, Britain might take over Louisiana before French troops arrived.

The French provided the United States with naval support against the British during the American Revolutionary War.

rival nations might begin fighting again. Neither man wanted to see Americans caught in the middle.

Jefferson was deeply troubled. But he did not speak out against Napoléon. Jefferson was fond of France. He had lived there for nearly five years as a diplomat. Many Americans considered France a friend too. It had supported the US cause during the American Revolutionary War (1775–1783). The United States had won its independence from Britain during the war.

Jefferson and Madison decided that diplomacy would be the best way to learn Napoléon's plans for

Robert Livingston, *center*, meets with French representatives.

Louisiana. On February 24, 1801, Jefferson asked Robert Livingston to become the US minister to France. Livingston had years of political experience.

News from Paris

On December 3, 1801, Livingston arrived in Paris. Over the next 18 months, he wrote many letters to Jefferson and Madison. The letters showed how difficult his situation was. He often spoke with Napoléon's minister of foreign affairs, Charles Maurice de Talleyrand. Talleyrand skillfully avoided Livingston's questions.

The French kept Jefferson on edge. In February 1802, Jefferson learned that Napoléon had put together a force of 20,000 men. Jefferson once again found himself trying to guess Napoléon's next move. But the men did not sail for Louisiana. They sailed first for Saint-Domingue in the Caribbean.

France's Plans for Louisiana

The movement of troops worried Jefferson. He wrote to Livingston on April 18, 1802. His letter warned that if France took New Orleans, the United States would need to appeal immediately to

PERSPECTIVES
French Expansion

Napoléon wanted to create a new French empire that stretched from the West Indies to the Mississippi Valley. His plans did not go smoothly. Slaves rebelled in the French colony of Saint-Domingue. Napoléon sent troops to regain control. His brother-in-law, General Charles Leclerc, led them. But a disease killed most of the men. This huge loss forced Napoléon to give up his dreams for an empire in the New World.

Britain. Jefferson did not want to ally with Britain. But if the US government failed to protect the Mississippi River, Jefferson knew it could lead to more problems. Western settlers might choose to separate from the United States. The river was very important to them.

The situation was delicate. Jefferson considered his next move carefully. He turned to a friend for help, former French diplomat Pierre Du Pont de Nemours. Jefferson asked Du Pont to explain the American position to France. Du Pont did not think it was wise to challenge Napoléon. Instead he suggested that Jefferson try to buy part of Louisiana from France. Jefferson took Du Pont's advice. On May 1, 1802, Jefferson sent a message to Livingston. He was told to find out how much France wanted for New Orleans and the Floridas. Jefferson did not know France did not hold the Floridas.

Jefferson also told Livingston to write letters to French officials. He was to make Louisiana sound unattractive. But the French government stalled talks with Livingston. Months passed.

Then, in September 1802, Jefferson heard that Napoléon had 3,000 men in Holland ready to set sail. Jefferson wondered how long it would be before the French came to New Orleans. After two months, Jefferson heard from Livingston. He had not yet convinced France to set a price for New Orleans.

EXPLORE ONLINE

The focus in Chapter Two is the difficulty Jefferson had determining what Napoléon's plans were for Louisiana. It also covers Livingston's negotiations with Napoléon's representatives. As you know, every source is different. How is the information given on the website below different from the information provided in the chapter? What information is the same? How do the two sources present information differently? What can you learn from this website?

Letter from Livingston to Madison
mycorelibrary.com/thomas-jefferson

CHAPTER THREE

CONTROL OF NEW ORLEANS

By the fall of 1802, France had still not taken control of Louisiana. But Jefferson's problems in the territory only grew. On October 16, 1802, he learned that Spanish official Juan Morales shut the Port of New Orleans to US goods. Jefferson thought of the boats loaded with tobacco, flour, and corn that sailed to New Orleans each day. They were important to the country's trade.

The Port of New Orleans was crucial for shipping goods to the coast of the United States.

Farmers needed to be able to ship their goods, such as cotton, to make a living.

Farmers called on their president to take action. They felt the closure was unfair. It also threatened their livelihoods. Reports claimed 20,000 men were ready to take the city by force. The farmers demanded that Jefferson and Congress protect their rights.

Congress quickly met to discuss the ban. Federalist members thought Napoléon was behind the port closure. They accused Jefferson of not giving them enough information about France's actions in Louisiana. On January 11, 1803, Congress asked Jefferson for any documents he had on Spain's sale of Louisiana to France. They wanted to see the conditions of the deal.

Representatives expressed concern about the length of time from when the agreement between France and Spain was made and when it came to light. Jefferson sent Congress a message. He asked the House to have faith in his government. But some members said the president was ignoring his duties. They asked why he had not demanded an explanation from his ministers in France or Spain about the situation in New Orleans.

Jefferson had hinted to his supporters in Congress that diplomacy with France would cost money. On January 11, 1803, General Samuel Smith of Maryland suggested that the House set aside $2 million. It could be used to buy New Orleans. The next day a committee recommended the United

Jefferson signed a bill allowing a US militia to be ready to take New Orleans. But he hoped the issue could be resolved peacefully.

States begin talks with France and Spain. But by February, Congress had lost patience. The Spanish had still not canceled Morales's order. New Orleans was still off limits to Americans.

A Federalist senator took action. He introduced a bill giving the president the right to raise a militia of 50,000 men. He wanted Jefferson to use the men to take New Orleans. But a more peaceful solution won out. On February 25, a motion passed allowing for 80,000 men to be ready. But they would be used only if talks with France failed. Jefferson signed the bill three days later.

The Second Envoy

Jefferson needed to gain US citizens' rights to trade through New Orleans. He asked James Monroe to help Livingston talk with the French. Monroe was Jefferson's friend. He was also well liked in the West. Westerners saw the nomination as proof that the president had their interests in mind. Congress quickly approved the appointment.

Livingston and Monroe meet with a French representative.

Before Monroe left, Jefferson spoke with his presidential cabinet. The US Constitution made no mention of adding land to the country. Jefferson now thought the purchase might be illegal. Attorney General Levi Lincoln suggested adding new land to existing states. He said this allowed Jefferson to make the purchase. Secretary of the Treasury Albert Gallatin told Jefferson the deal would be legal regardless.

Jefferson gave Monroe permission to offer France up to $10 million for New Orleans and West Florida. "All eyes, all hopes, are now fixed on you," Jefferson wrote. "On the event of this mission depends the future destinies of this republic."

Monroe reached Paris on April 12, 1803. He was amazed to find that the situation had changed. Napoléon now wanted to sell all of Louisiana. The Floridas, which still belonged to Spain, were not part of the deal. Talks moved quickly. Napoléon needed money fast to fight his upcoming wars with Britain and Austria.

PERSPECTIVES
Napoléon's Decision

Napoléon did not want the British to have Louisiana. They had already taken much of Canada from France. By selling Louisiana to the United States, Napoléon prevented the British from gaining land and resources. He believed someday the United States would become a good friend to France.

Uncharted Territory

French and US representatives could not agree on Louisiana's exact borders. There were none at the time. Louisiana had never been fully explored by Americans or Europeans. There were no complete maps. Talleyrand told Livingston the United States had to take the territory as the French received it. Livingston and Monroe accepted the terms and signed the treaty. The United States would not agree with Spain about Louisiana's boundaries until 16 years after the deal.

The United States and France came to an agreement by the end of the month. The United States would pay France $15 million for Louisiana. This would be equal to more than $200 million today. Part of this money was for US claims against France for damages during the French and Indian War. On May 22, Napoléon approved the deal. The envoys hurried to write to tell Jefferson the news. The United States had doubled in size at a cost of four cents per acre.

In January 1803, Jefferson sent a secret message to Congress. It laid out plans for Louisiana. The following excerpt discusses Jefferson's main goals in relating to Native Americans:

> *First: to encourage them to abandon hunting, to apply to the raising stock, to agriculture and domestic manufacture, and thereby prove to themselves that less land and labor will maintain them in this, better than in their former mode of living. The extensive forests necessary in the hunting life, will then become useless, and they will see advantage in exchanging them for the means of improving their farms. . . . Secondly: to multiply trading houses among them. . . . In leading them to agriculture, to manufactures, and civilization; in bringing together their and our settlements, and in preparing them ultimately to participate in the benefits of our governments, I trust and believe we are acting for their greatest good.*
>
> Source: Thomas Jefferson. "Jefferson's Secret Message to Congress." Library of Congress. US Government, n.d. Web. Accessed July 1, 2015.

Point of View

Jefferson often talked about bringing "civilization" to Native Americans. According to this passage, how did he want to change the Native American way of life? Do you agree with his reasoning? Why or why not?

AN AMERICAN TERRITORY

Jefferson received the good news on July 3, 1803. It was unexpected, but Jefferson saw it as a big opportunity for his country. He announced the purchase to the public the next day. But not everyone was pleased.

Jefferson's political opponents, the Federalists, attacked him and the purchase. They accused him of spending too much money for wilderness. They

Though the United States and France came to an agreement, the deal still needed to be approved by Congress.

Jefferson was known for upholding the Constitution. He was worried he might be going against it with the Louisiana Purchase.

wondered how the United States could defend such a large piece of land. Some said a country so big would never stay together. But many Americans saw the treaty as a reason to celebrate. They were excited the country had grown so large.

The crisis was over. But doubts swirled through Jefferson's mind. His reputation was built on sticking to the US Constitution. He believed a president could only take actions allowed by the Constitution. He had argued this since entering politics. Now he had bought land. The Constitution did not say a president could buy land.

Jefferson made a suggestion to his cabinet. He wanted to create an amendment to the Constitution. It would make it legal for him to purchase land. Madison, Lincoln, and Gallatin did not think an amendment was needed. Jefferson decided he would write one.

A letter from France changed his mind. Monroe and Livingston wrote that Napoléon was growing impatient. Jefferson's cabinet told him that an amendment would take time to pass. Any delays in passing the treaty might result in Napoléon calling off the deal. Jefferson could not take this risk.

Congress Approves

Jefferson listened to his cabinet. He submitted the purchase to Congress for approval. Though he had objections, Jefferson thought the benefits for the country were more important.

On October 17, 1803, Congress met to approve the deal. The president sent a message to the senators and representatives. He explained how the

Louisiana Purchase promoted peace and friendship between the United States and France. He assured Congress the purchase would be paid off in 15 years. Jefferson believed he had done all he could. Now he hoped Congress would approve the purchase quickly.

Jefferson again found himself being criticized. Some senators did not agree with the purchase. A Federalist senator accused Jefferson of taking the Senate's approval for granted. In the House of Representatives, members debated the constitutionality of the purchase. Some reminded Jefferson that he had said the government only had powers that were in the Constitution. Though critics raised this issue, they were not able to pursue it.

Senators knew that the majority of Americans were pleased with Jefferson's decision. On October 20, the Senate passed the purchase by a vote of 24 to 7. Two days later, the House approved funding for the purchase. Jefferson was relieved. Louisiana officially changed hands on December 20.

Napoléon's representative officially transfers the land to Captain Amos Stoddard of the US Army in 1804.

Lewis and Clark Go West

Jefferson's thoughts turned to exploration. He had already asked Congress to fund an expedition. Part of this journey would now be on land belonging to the United States. Jefferson asked his former secretary, Meriwether Lewis, to lead the group. Lewis asked his friend William Clark to help him lead the trip. The group became known as the Corps of Discovery.

Jefferson played a key role in planning the trip. He wanted the team to find a river route to the Pacific

- 55-foot (17-meter) keelboat
- 35 oars
- 150 yards (140 m) of cloth to be oiled and sewn into tents
- 2 horses
- mosquito curtains
- 10.5 pounds (5 kg) of fishing hooks and fishing lines
- 193 pounds (87.5 kg) of "portable soup"
- 45 flannel shirts
- 20 coats
- 30 stockings
- 15 pairs wool overalls
- 15 Prototype Model 1803 muzzle-loading .54-caliber rifles
- 420 pounds (191 kg) of sheet lead for bullets
- 176 pounds (80 kg) of gunpowder packed in 52 lead canisters
- hand compass
- 1 telescope
- 3 thermometers
- 1 portable microscope
- 20 pounds (9 kg) of assorted beads, mostly blue
- ivory combs
- dictionary (4-volume)
- tables for finding longitude and latitude

Supplies for the Journey

Explorers Lewis and Clark set out to chart the Louisiana Territory in 1804. This list shows some of Lewis and Clark's preparations for the journey west. How do you think they decided to purchase these items with little knowledge of the area?

Ocean. He wanted them to learn more about plants, animals, and Native American tribes of the West.

In the spring of 1804, the team set out from Saint Louis to explore the northern part of the Louisiana Purchase. It was a very exciting time. No one knew what they would discover. They encountered many trials, from fast-flowing rivers and snow to the Rocky Mountains. But by November 1805, the Pacific Ocean was in view.

The Corps began their long journey home the following spring. In September 1806, they arrived back in Saint Louis. They reported their findings to Jefferson. Their achievements delighted the president. Jefferson devoted an entire room in his home to the team's discoveries. He put fossils, bones, and Native American objects on display.

The Northwest Passage

Jefferson believed the Corps would find a water route to cross the continent. He thought the route could be used to increase trade. Many explorers had hoped to find a way of connecting the Atlantic and Pacific Oceans. For more than 400 years, explorers searched without success. Many of these expeditions ended in disaster. It was not until 1906 that a Norwegian explorer completed a trip from the Atlantic to the Pacific by navigating waters in northern Canada. The route was known as the Northwest Passage. But it was too far north to be used for regular transportation.

Settling the West

The explorers did not find a water route to the West Coast. But they did make a path to the Pacific. Their discoveries and tales of adventure made many people excited about the West. The Louisiana Purchase encouraged thousands of Americans to move across the Mississippi River. Many thought God wanted the country to grow to the West. But the territory was already home to hundreds of different Native American tribes. The expansion into the West was often terrible for Native Americans, who had their lands taken from them.

The population of the United States grew from 5 million in 1800 to more than 23 million by 1850. People from around the world came to the country looking for opportunity.

By the 1900s, the Louisiana Purchase was part of 15 states. The nation stretched from the Atlantic in the east to the Pacific in the west. Thomas Jefferson's dream had come true.

FURTHER EVIDENCE

Chapter Four discusses Jefferson's uncertainties about the Louisiana Purchase. What was one of the main points of this chapter? What evidence is included to support this point? Read the article on the website below. Does the information on the website support the main point of the chapter? What new evidence does it present?

The Louisiana Purchase and the Constitution
mycorelibrary.com/thomas-jefferson

IMPORTANT DATES

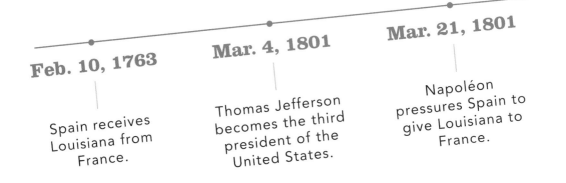

Feb. 10, 1763

Spain receives Louisiana from France.

Mar. 4, 1801

Thomas Jefferson becomes the third president of the United States.

Mar. 21, 1801

Napoléon pressures Spain to give Louisiana to France.

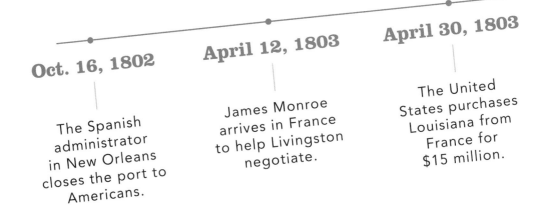

Oct. 16, 1802

The Spanish administrator in New Orleans closes the port to Americans.

April 12, 1803

James Monroe arrives in France to help Livingston negotiate.

April 30, 1803

The United States purchases Louisiana from France for $15 million.

Mar. 29, 1801

Rufus King alerts Thomas Jefferson to the secret deal between Spain and France.

Dec. 3, 1801

Thomas Jefferson's envoy, Robert Livingston, arrives in France to begin negotiations with the French.

Feb. 1802

Napoléon's troops arrive in the French colony of Saint-Dominigue to put down a slave revolt.

Oct. 20, 1803

The Senate approves the Louisiana Purchase.

May 14, 1804

The Corps of Discovery begins an expedition from Saint Louis, Missouri, to the Pacific Ocean.

1809

Thomas Jefferson retires and returns to his home, Monticello, in Virginia.

STOP AND THINK

Say What?

Studying historical events, such as the Louisiana Purchase, can mean learning new vocabulary. Find five words in this book you have never seen or heard before. Use a dictionary to find out what they mean. Then write each meaning in your own words and use each word in a sentence.

Tell the Tale

Chapter One discusses settlers living in the Ohio Valley who used the Mississippi River. Imagine you are a settler dependent on the river for transportation and trade. Write 200 words about sailing your flatboat to New Orleans. Be sure to include details about the people you meet along the way, sights, sounds, and your experiences in New Orleans.

Take a Stand

Chapter Three discusses the closure of the port of New Orleans. Some settlers and members of Congress wanted to use force to retake the city. Do you feel that their actions would have solved the crisis? Why or why not?

Dig Deeper

After reading this book, what questions do you still have about Thomas Jefferson? With an adult's help, find a few reliable sources that can help you answer your questions. Write a paragraph about what you learned.

GLOSSARY

amendment
a change to a country's constitution

cabinet
a group of advisers to the president

colony
people living in a territory ruled by another country

constitution
the belief and law of a nation

Democratic-Republican
a member of a political party that favored limiting the power of the central government

diplomacy
talks between countries by government officials

envoy
a messenger sent from one country to another

Federalist
a person belonging to a political party that believed in a strong central government

militia
a military force of civilians

treaty
a formal agreement between countries

LEARN MORE

Books

Dunn, Joeming. *Thomas Jefferson.* Edina, MN: Abdo Publishing, 2009.

Yasuda, Anita. *Westward Expansion of the United States: 1801–1861.* Minneapolis, MN: Abdo Publishing, 2014.

Zurn, Jon. *The Louisiana Purchase.* Edina, MN: Abdo Publishing, 2008.

Websites

To learn more about Presidential Perspectives, visit **booklinks.abdopublishing.com**. These links are routinely monitored and updated to provide the most current information available.

Visit **mycorelibrary.com** for additional free tools for teachers and students.

INDEX

ABOUT THE AUTHOR

Anita Yasuda is the author of more than 100 books for children. She lives with her family in Huntington Beach, California, where you can find her on most days walking her dog along the shore.